30 JOYFUL DAYS OF CREATIVITY

Copyright © 2023 Baffling Books Ltd.

All rights reserved.

ISBN: 9798392208012

30 JOYFUL DAYS OF CREATIVITY

AWAKEN YOUR INNER CREATIVE GENIUS IN JUST 30 DAYS

Christopher John

Baffling Books Ltd.

CONTENTS

	INTRODUCTION	1
1	WHAT CAN I STEAL?	3
2	THE AMAZING WHY	7
3	THE CRAZIEST SOLUTION	10
4	HOW CAN WE MAKE IT MORE...?	15
5	WHAT'S A SMALL, QUICK WIN?	18
6	WHAT DO I WANT TO SEE?	22
7	WHAT COULD MAKE THIS 10X AS GOOD?	26
8	RANDOM WORD TIME	31
9	BECOME A PROFESSIONAL	34
10	WHAT IF WE USED A DIFFERENT APPROACH?	36
11	JUST GET ON WITH IT	40
12	HOW CAN WE CUT AWAY ALL THE UNNECESSARY PARTS?	43
13	HOW CAN WE CHANGE OUR POINT OF VIEW?	45
14	WHAT WOULD MY HERO DO?	47
15	STOP BEING SUCH A HARSH CRITIC—PART 1	51
16	STOP BEING SUCH A HARSH CRITIC—PART 2	54
17	ARE YOU USING THESE THREE LOGICAL STEPS?	57
18	WHAT LESSONS CAN YOU APPLY FROM YOUR PAST?	61

19	WHAT IF YOU IMPOSED SEVERE CONSTRAINTS?	65
20	PICTURE THE END GOAL BUT GET IT RIGHT	68
21	WHAT IF WE WROTE OUR OWN RULES?	71
22	IDENTIFY YOUR PROBLEM. MAKE IT AN OPPORTUNITY.	75
23	BE THE HARSHEST CRITIC YOU CAN IMAGINE	78
24	WHAT COULD MAKE THIS SO GOOD, PEOPLE WILL WONDER HOW THEY LIVED WITHOUT IT?	81
25	WHERE ARE YOU SITUATED IN LIFE, CULTURE AND SOCIETY?	87
26	ARE YOU EXPERIENCING LIFE ENOUGH?	89
27	IN THE UPCOMING JOURNEY, WHAT IS THE PINNACLE MOMENT?	91
28	AM I CONNECTING TO OTHERS ON AN EMOTIONAL LEVEL?	94
29	HAVE YOU OVERCOME YOUR SELF-DOUBT?	98
30	ARE YOU BEING KIND TO OTHERS?	103
31	BONUS SECTION	106

"You can't use up creativity.

The more you use, the more you have."

Maya Angelou

INTRODUCTION

You can decide how to approach this. Either you pick a time during each day to open this book and learn that day's lesson, or you impatiently flick fast and furiously through the pages to find what you need right now. Both are great. Or maybe you stretch beyond the thirty days, or perhaps you decide to gobble it all up in a single sitting. Whichever way you choose, this book is useless to you as simply words on the page. It becomes useful only when you push hard to complete the tasks with the guidance it lays out. When you reflect and consider. When you research and write. When you think and when you apply yourself.

Now, if there's a single piece of advice in this book that changes the way you approach creativity, then this investment of time and money and energy will have been a success. And success in creativity can be a multiplier to other areas in your life and the lives of others. If your creative or engineering, scientific or business pursuits in any way impact other people, then this will be a transformative process you're about to go through that could impact the lives of many. You should approach your tasks now with the level of duty that demands.

1 WHAT CAN I STEAL?

"Good artists copy. Great artists steal."

Unknown

"Good artists copy. Great artists steal."

That quote has been attributed to many artists. But its original form, whatever it was, was very different. The quote evolved as it was repeated, and transformed, as one artist took it from another and changed it a little.

That is the nature of creativity. And you should understand that before going any further. Creativity is the act of combining existing things. By their combination, they become transformed.

This can be quite a mindset shift. Because it means you stop struggling to peer into some empty space above your head to pluck out an amazing insight. Instead, you look elsewhere. You look at what has gone before—the other creators and artists, scientists and engineers, entrepreneurs and entertainers. To find what they've done successfully, and copy.

And steal.

You learn from them what worked well and take it and make it your own. And sometimes that's pretty close to thievery. But what you're doing is analysis and assessment to find pieces with which to create something completely fresh. And to understand how and why these pieces work.

And this requires some action.

It's the first action, really, that you need to do in this odyssey of creativity on which you're about to embark.

So, take a moment to do some quick research. What's an example of something that's done really well in your field? Write it down below.

_____

_____

_____

_____

Got it? Good. Now, what is it about this example that's so good? What do you admire about it? Write it down below.

_____

_____

_____

_____

Now, be specific. What's the feature or characteristic that you can learn from? Write it here.

_____

_____

_____

_____

You just took the first step in understanding the brush strokes and moves that underlie your craft. You must steal like a thief to learn from the best. And even if you only have a minute to spare, if you haven't done it yet go online and find something you like, spot one element, and make a mental note of what makes it good. Do this now, that's your task!

It's in the practice of doing this whenever you are faced with a creative challenge, that you will become good. If you can't have a master to study beneath, then this is the next best thing. You deconstruct the work of others you admire, to help you understand your craft.

And here's the kicker, folks. This process of collecting great works and analyzing them never ends. You must keep stealing and learning if you want to be great. That is where we start.

So, let's make a small gesture of commitment.

I _____

Promise that when I am faced with a creative challenge, I will consult other existing work.

I will see what they did and understand why it worked.

I will consider using elements that worked well and combine them in new ways.

I will do this mindfully, constantly learning, and improving my skills.

Signed:

_____

2 THE AMAZING WHY

"The only way to do great work is to love what you do."

Steve Jobs

Why is it worth spending time trying to be more creative? What could you possibly get from it? How might it change the time you spend on this planet?

This all might depend on what you're planning to do. What are you planning to create in the next ten years of your life? In the next twenty? What are you hoping to bring into this world?

Because if you can improve your creative process just 10%, what sort of difference might that make?

It's this line of thought you should consider now. If you pause to dwell on what the implications of a small improvement are, it might start to give you some insight into the implications of a huge improvement.

Would you benefit from an enormous improvement in how you approach creative projects?

Obviously, you're a one-of-a-kind vessel for the creative process, capable of producing something that is uniquely *you*. Something that comes from your personality and life experiences. But it's often easy to forget the unique position you hold and why it matters.

Let's start with finishing this sentence:

It's worth spending time trying to improve my creative process, because:

_____

_____

_____

_____

Got it? Great. Now, ask yourself why you want that outcome? What's driving you to achieve it? Take a moment to really dwell on that. Write your deep, personal reason here.

_____

_____

_____

_____

Why do you want your creation to stand out? Is it because you want to change your life? Show the world what you're made of? Have fun and unleash your creativity? Whatever the reason, you need to feel it deep down in your bones. You need to associate the effort it will take to produce an outstanding creation with the amazing feeling of purpose and goodness that comes when it's all done. Take a deep breath and feel that creative charge course through your body.

Now that you know what you want to achieve and why, it's time to take it to the next level. Ask yourself, "What am I willing to do to achieve it?" Are you willing to put in the hard work, push yourself out of your comfort zone, and take risks to make your creation outstanding? You're going to need to go the extra mile, so ask yourself, "How far am I willing to go to make this happen?"

So, remember your deep personal reason, and use it to push you on.

3 THE CRAZIEST SOLUTION

"All progress depends on the unreasonable man."

George Bernard Shaw

Alright, folks, now it's time to talk about the crazy stuff. You know, the things that make you go, "Wait, what?! That's insane!" So, what's the craziest solution to this problem? Think about the creative challenge that lies ahead of you whether it's composing a song that tugs at our heartstrings or developing a new app that's un-put-downable, what's the craziest solution that still solves your challenge?

What's the craziest solution? I want you to answer that question right now, right off the top of your head.

_____

_____

_____

_____

Great job! But now we need to develop that crazy idea a bit more. Let's think about what we can extract from this crazy solution.

For example, let's say we're writing a diet book. An outlandish solution might be to have a diet coach come and stay with you in your home (like, what?!). But we can take an aspect of that idea and adapt the diet book tips to be more conversational and encouraging, like you have your own personal coach cheering you on.

Or let's say we're working on a new recipe. An impractical solution could be to analyze the taste profiles of a thousand different recipes. But we can extract the idea of analyzing a few recipes ourselves and building up a database of what works and what doesn't.

But now, let's take it up a notch. What's the most off-the-wall, boundary-free solution you can think of? Don't worry if it's completely impractical, this is just the starting point. But to really do this right, we need to ask ourselves: what is the true goal of the thing we're creating? For a mystery thriller, it might be to enrapture, captivate, shock, entertain, befuddle, amuse. For a car design, it might be to make people fall in love with its beauty.

So, what's the true goal of your creative work? Write it down now.

_____

_____

_____

_____

Now, what's the craziest, most out-there solution you can think of that might actually achieve that true goal? Don't hold back, let your imagination run wild.

_____

_____

_____

_____

Alright, now let's extract something useful from that crazy idea. What can you take from it that you might actually be able to implement in a realistic way? Maybe it's a small detail or a big concept, but there's always something you can use. Write it down.

_____

_____

_____

_____

But wait, there's more! Now that you've completed that exercise above, let's go in a different direction now. What's something so crazy that it would shock people, but in a good way? For our diet book, maybe we decide to give it away for free (say what?!). Obviously, that's not really feasible, but maybe we can give away some other helpful resources for free. Or for our recipe, maybe we decide to make the world's largest cake (uh, yeah right). But we could still have an "extreme" cake theme, with huge layers and bold flavors.

So, what's your shockingly crazy idea? Write it down.

_____

_____

_____

_____

And finally, what can you extract from this idea? How can you use it to make your creative work even better? Write it down.

_____

_____

_____

_____

The goal here is to take something away from this exercise, no matter how small. So, make sure you do.

4 HOW CAN WE MAKE IT MORE...?

"Far away in the sunshine are my highest aspirations. I may not reach them, but I can look up and see their beauty, believe in them, and try to follow where they lead."

Louisa May Alcott

It's time to talk about how to make your project more, well, whatever descriptive word you want it to be! Is it fun? Emotional? Appealing? Fast? Blue? Sustainable? Powerful? You pick the word, and let's get started.

So, let's say we want to make an advertisement more powerful. How do we do that? It could be by making it more attention-grabbing or emotionally appealing. Once we've settled on our word, we may need to get more specific.

If we're talking about an ad, we should look at its features and ask ourselves, "How can we change the color, contrast, facial expressions, or message to raise its attention-grabbing or emotional power?" Don't be afraid to think outside the box and explore different ways to achieve your goal.

Now, here's the deal: the first solution that comes to mind may not be the best one. But if it is, then high-five, you're killing it. If not, try this trick: ask yourself, "What if we had no choice but to make it more _____?" Fill in the blank with your chosen word and see what comes to mind.

If the descriptive feature you're choosing is something positive that your project should have, then it's worth pursuing until you have a solution you can implement.

So, what's your chosen word? Write it here.

_____

_____

_____

_____

Now consider what you need to do to make it more of that. Let's do this, people! Write it here.

_____

_____

_____

_____

Now you can repeat this with different words—different characteristics of your work you wish to improve.

5 WHAT'S A SMALL, QUICK WIN?

"The journey of a thousand miles begins with a single step."

Lao Tzu

Alright, folks, listen up because I'm about to drop some knowledge on how to push through those grey clouds and get into the zone. We've all been there, struggling to get into that flow state where everything just clicks. But fear not, because I've got some tips to help you out.

First things first, let's talk about flow. It's that magical state where you're fully immersed in an activity that challenges you just enough to keep you focused but not overwhelmed. But here's the thing, to get into flow, you have to get those moves going. That's right, every flow state starts with one small move, whether it's hitting a ball or typing a single word.

But wait, there's more. You can't just rely on your skills and the activity itself to get into flow. Your environmental, mental, emotional, and physical conditions all play a role. So put down that phone, drink some water, eat a snack (or don't), and get rid of any distractions. And most importantly, find joy in those small achievements, because if each move annoys you, flow will be harder to find.

So, remember to get into flow starts with one move. To get the flow state going you need to string those moves together. To string them along naturally you need to enjoy them from one to the next. To enjoy them you need to realize what you're doing is a specific activity—a special unique act—which is important to do for your overall creative challenge.

Whether it's copying and pasting for your research, filling in some numbers into an excel spreadsheet, or even going through the motions on the tasks in this book, you should be able to label that distinct activity as one of the activities it takes to become creatively brilliant, and achieve your creative dreams. When you've been able to clearly distinguish and label all the different tasks associated with your big creative projects, and frame them as skills you get better at, rather than burdens you bear, you'll be well placed to get into flow even in the most mundane-seeming of tasks.

So go ahead, take that tiny step, and then take the next one. And the next. And before you know it, you'll be in the zone, stringing those moves together like a boss. And when you finally finish that big scary project, you'll look back and realize it all started with one small move.

...

Now we've got flow out the way, let's talk about how to tackle those big scary projects. Start with the smallest, quickest, easiest step you can take to get a micro win. A win that's small, easy but high-five-worthy. Got it? Good. Now break that down into an even smaller step. And then break that down again. Keep breaking it down until it seems doable, until you can imagine that small victory and feel it in your bones.

Let's do that now. Imagine you're faced with a seemingly insurmountable project in front of you that you just can't bear to face. Get a real one in your mind if you can. What's the smallest step you can take? The smallest quick win? Got it? Write it down.

_____

_____

_____

_____

Now take that small quick win and break it down again into an even smaller step. If it was submitting an online form maybe a smaller step is to type in your name on the form for example. Got it? Write it here.

_____

_____

_____

_____

And now we're going to take this one step further. Into the land that we could call "useful absurdity". Break that tiny step down into an even smaller step to make. Like, say, moving your finger towards the right keys on the keyboard. Got it?

Write it here.

_____

_____

_____

_____

Now this step is where you should focus all your motivation and energy. On this tiny seemingly insignificant step. Get to it!

6 WHAT DO I WANT TO SEE?

"You are not your circumstances. You are your possibilities. If you know that, you can do anything."

Oprah Winfrey

Let's help get your creative juices flowing. So, tell me, what do YOU want to see? No, no, no, say it like you mean it! What do you WANT to see? What do you want to SEE?

Now, let's talk about your finished work. What do you want to see in it? Maybe there are four things that come to mind. Let's start with one thing, just to keep it simple.

Identify that one thing that you want that will shine out in your work. Maybe it's a killer joke, a dramatic plot twist, or the perfect shade of pink. Whatever it is, write it down.

_____

_____

_____

Now, let's figure out what it will take to get there. What steps do you need to take to bring that one thing to life? Write those down too.

_____

_____

_____

_____

But wait, there's more! Ask yourself what unusual activity that you don't regularly do it will take to actually see that one thing come to fruition. Maybe you need to collaborate with someone, research some more, or just plain old practice. Write it down here.

_____

_____

_____

_____

Now, that's one. What's the next thing you want to see in your completed work?

_____

_____

_____

_____

How will you have to go beyond your regular steps to get that?

_____

_____

_____

_____

Excellent. Consider doing this for all the important parts of your project. Keep going with this process until you've nailed down the exact steps that will get you to your end goal. And don't forget to make checklists along the way! These lists will be your best friend throughout your creative journey and will help you make sure you've hit all your marks at the end.

So go forth, my friends, and create something amazing. And remember, always ask yourself: What do I want to see? What do I WANT to see? What do I want to SEE?

7 WHAT COULD MAKE THIS 10X AS GOOD?

"Creativity takes courage."

Henri Matisse

It's time to ask ourselves a question that can supercharge the outcomes of our project.

What would make this ten times as good?

But you must put yourself in your audience's shoes and think about what would make them go "Wow, this is unbelievably better!" Whether it's a book, a YouTube video, or a complex design, you need to figure out what new feature or element would make your work stand out from the rest.

Write that down now. Rack your mind and think what would make this 10X better for them.

_____

_____

_____

_____

Got it? Excellent well done. Now if you happen to have some, say, engineering challenge, you could still do this exercise but change being 10X better for your audience to 10X more efficient, fast or whatever metric truly counts. So, let's go through this again.

Now, if ten times seems a bit too unrealistic for you, go ahead and choose a number that makes sense for your field and your brain. One way is to think big and be creative. Who knows, maybe starting with the unfeasible will lead you to a breakthrough idea! In fact, that's actually exactly how this works. But you also have the option to be a bit more grounded with this one, it's totally up to you. It might be quite feasible to make something twice as good, so you could try both—a big number and a small one.

So, let's get started. Pick a number and ask yourself, "What could make it X times as good?" Don't hold back, be as crazy and creative as you want to be when developing solutions. But also remember to think about what the top examples in your field accomplish and how they do what they do.

Once you have your answer, write down why this would make it X times as good.

_____

_____

_____

_____

Now from this possibly outlandish solution, what elements might you realistically apply to your project? Write that here.

_____

_____

_____

_____

And if you're feeling extra ambitious, go ahead and repeat this process with all the parts of the project that really matter. Trust me, it's worth it. So go out there and make something ten times as good!

CONGRATULATIONS

Well, well, well, look who made it through all seven challenges! You deserve a round of applause, my friend. But before we move on, let's take a moment to reflect on what you've accomplished. First things first, give yourself a pat on the back and say "Well done!" And really mean it. Whether you skipped ahead or procrastinated for years before starting, trying to become a more creative problem solver is a worthy use of your time, and you should be proud of yourself for taking this step.

Now, to keep the momentum going, you need to celebrate your successes, no matter how small they may seem. And believe it or not I'm actually talking about simply just a fist pump and a "woohoo." I'm talking about releasing those sweet, sweet "celebration" chemicals in your brain by really feeling it when you complete an exercise in this book. So go ahead and dance around the room, high-five yourself, or even do a victory lap around the block. Just make sure you're celebrating every step of the way. You need to experience that celebratory release. Trust me on this – that small positivity will help you later, so don't skip this. Feel awesome about yourself right now.

Speaking of steps, let's move on to reflection number two. Reading these words and implementing them into new habits of action and thought are two completely different things. You can't just absorb information and expect to become a creative master overnight. It takes work, dedication, and most importantly, forming new habits. So choose one of the seven creative insights we've covered and make a conscious effort to turn it into a habit.

Now, don't go crazy and try to establish all seven habits at once. That's a recipe for disaster, my friend. Instead, pick one and stick with it until it becomes automatic. Need a refresher on what those insights were? Here's a quick recap:

1. I will steal from...
2. This matters to me, because...
3. A crazy solution would be...
4. I will make it more _____
5. My next small, quick win will be...
6. I will go the extra mile to reach my vision by...
7. I will make this 10X as good by...

Choose the one that speaks to you the most and start incorporating it into your daily routine. And don't worry if it sounds a bit "mumbo-jumbo self-help-like." These changes can make a real impact on your creative life, especially when you're feeling stuck or unmotivated.

So, my friend, you have a choice to make. You can either keep reading this book, or you can put it down, take those notes, and start implementing these habits into your life. The decision is yours, but remember, the only way to go from amateur to master is through daily habits. And with that, I'll leave you to it. Good luck, and may the creative force be with you!

8 RANDOM WORD TIME

"Everything is a remix."

Kirby Ferguson

Okay, so picture this: there's a freaking helicopter outside, an ant crawling on my desk, a picture of an antenna on my screen, and dogs howling like they're auditioning for a horror movie outside my window. And then, out of nowhere, I'm hit with the mental image of a Roman army centurion uniform and a cute little bunny rabbit. What is going on here?!

Random thoughts. Random objects. Random ideas. But you know what? That's the beauty of creativity. If you can't come up with something out of thin air, just take a look around you and find inspiration in the randomness.

Here's the deal: you're going to take that random idea or object and find something within it that you can use in your creative project. And trust me, there's so much complexity and beauty in this world that you can find something interesting in just about anything.

Got your random thought or object? Write it here.

_____

_____

_____

_____

Great! Now it's time to analyze its features. What makes this uniquely the item in question that it is? This tells you the features, characteristics—even operations—of that object or idea and these are what you're about to apply to your existing craft.

So say you choose Penguins. And you're writing a song. Well you could say Penguins are black and white, or light and dark. And you could make a powerful song that contrasted a really bright happy image with a devastatingly sad one. You can take any features and use them in this fashion. And the more you know about the item or concept you choose the better. Say you're a scientist grappling with a complex problem. You might want to choose a completely separate domain from your specialism but one that nonetheless has deep complexity within it, and take some unusual concepts and structures and apply them to your field. Whatever your creative field, write some of the features of your random object or concept here.

_____

_____

_____

_____

Choose one feature from the above and apply it to your field.

_____

_____

_____

_____

9 BECOME A PROFESSIONAL

"Don't loaf and invite inspiration; light out after it with a club, and if you don't get it you will nonetheless get something that looks remarkably like it."

Jack London

Alright, listen up folks! We're going to talk about something serious. I know, I know, we all want to be creative and have fun, but if you're serious about this, you have to be a professional. What does that mean, you ask? It means you treat this like a career choice. Your work, your business, your job—this is it! You have deadlines, you have finished products to deliver, and you have to take it seriously.

You wouldn't show up two hours late to work or a meeting without the main item everyone's expecting, right? So why would you do that with your creative projects? These are the projects that matter most to you, so don't be unprofessional with them. You have to be responsible and deliver.

Being a professional means you spend the time to get good. You do the research, you practice, you develop your skills. You put in the time to support your creative ambitions. Are you ready to become a professional about this, or not? If not, put this book down and come back when you are.

So, let's get serious, people. If you're in, you're in. And if you're not, well, there's always amateur hour at the local coffee shop. But if you want to make it in the big leagues, you have to be a pro. Let's do this!

10 WHAT IF WE USED A DIFFERENT APPROACH?

"Many of life's failures are people who did not realize how close they were to success when they gave up."

Thomas Edison

Alright, my fellow creative adventurers, let's get ready to shake things up! This one's going to be fun, I promise. We're going to take a completely different approach, like a boss!

So, think about it. What's missing from your current approach? Is there something that's been holding you back, keeping you from reaching your creative goals? Write it down, own it, and let's move on to the good stuff.

Write here, what's missing from your creative work?

_____

_____

_____

Now, let's get crazy and think of a new and utterly different approach that could give you what you're missing. Go ahead, let your imagination run wild! Think outside the box, break the rules, and come up with something that's going to blow your mind.

What's an utterly, completely different approach that would solve that missing issue?

_____

_____

_____

_____

Now, that might give you some interesting ideas but let's take a step back, and up, and simply ask, "what's a way to approach your whole project that would make people think you're a bit mad, but would actually still bring a big benefit?"

_____

_____

_____

_____

Now, answer, "what part can I take from that which I can feasibly apply to my work?"

_____

_____

_____

_____

But here's the thing, my friends. It might not be easy. It might take some extra effort, and it might even mean doing things you don't necessarily want to do. But hey, nothing great ever comes from staying in our comfort zones, am I right?

So, let's break it down. Take that new approach and break it into its smallest first step. And I mean, like, really small. We're talking baby steps here, people. Write what that action is here.

_____

_____

_____

_____

And then, without wasting any time, do it. Do it as fast as you possibly can. Drop the book, go for it, and let's see your new approach in action!

And as you're taking that leap, pay attention to how it makes you feel. Embrace the emotions, my friends. If it gives you some benefit, make sure you feel that positivity. You're going to rock it, I just know it!

So, let's do this. Take that first step, and let's see the momentum build up. Who knows, this new approach might just be the game-changer you've been waiting for. Get ready to slay those creative goals like a boss! You got this! Now go, go, go!

11 JUST GET ON WITH IT

"You can't just sit there and wait for people to give you that golden dream. You've got to get out there and make it happen for yourself."

Diana Ross

Alright, my creative friend, let's get down to business.
We both know you've been putting this off for way too long.
But the good news is, all you need to do right now is take the tiniest, most positive step forward.
I'm talking baby steps here, folks. Like, literally just taking a deep breath and saying "I got this".
Or maybe opening up your laptop and staring at your project for a minute.
Just do something, anything, to get the ball rolling.
And when you feel yourself getting distracted by the siren call

of Netflix or Instagram, don't panic.

Instead, train yourself to recognize those moments and snap out of them like a ninja.

Seriously, it's a skill. And you can totally master it with practice.

So, if you're reading this and thinking "oh crap, that's me right now", take a deep breath and repeat after me: "Let's do this".

The trick really is to see it as a huge win. A huge quick celebration-worthy, happiness-inducing, outstanding win to even move one inch in that direction. To do even the very first step. That's one mindset shift that you should be taking in these pages. From one activity to the next, each one should fill you with optimism and joy.

If you notice yourself straying away from your task—maybe you found yourself standing in front of the fridge—at these moments think, "OK what's the next quick win I could get from my creative project that would make me instantly feel a little happy?" And so my creative friend the advice is simply snap out of your wandering and get back to it!

Let's prepare ahead of these moments.

Fill this in with one of the moments that's likely to come in the future when you're distracted away from your task. It could be when you're suddenly doom-scrolling or bingeing too much Netflix!

When I am next:

_____

_____

_____

_____

And now, write the positive thought you will have that will help snap you round back on task.

I will remember:

_____

_____

_____

_____

And this will help me get back on task because:

_____

_____

_____

_____

12 HOW CAN WE CUT AWAY ALL THE UNNECESSARY PARTS?

"Every block of stone has a statue inside it, and it is the task of the sculptor to discover it."

Michelangelo

You ready? Let's do this!

Great art is all about removing the unnecessary. It's like sculpting—the statue only appears when you chisel away all the excess stone. So, let's channel our inner Michelangelo and ask, "What can we cut out? What's not necessary?" But here's the kicker: to actually do this, you need to see your work. Visualize it or, even better, lay it out in front of you. Then point to the thing that's not needed and say, "You're outta here, buddy!"

Identify one thing that's not needed in your work.

_____

_____

_____

_____

Boom! Now, let's get rid of it. Is it a word? A color? An image? A function? A section? A button? Chop it out like it's a bad ex's number from your phone. Find a way for your work to exist without it, and then reflect on how you've made it better and why.

Write how it's better without it.

_____

_____

_____

_____

In some cases, it might be a bit tricky, but keep cutting and assessing until it still has the same character.

Now, if you make this a habit, it'll become a powerful tool in your creative arsenal. So go on, start choppin'! People will be thanking you for it.

13 HOW CAN WE CHANGE OUR POINT OF VIEW?

"If you change the way you look at things, the things you look at change."

Wayne Dyer

Hey there, creative genius! Let's talk about your customers or audience. What do they care about? How do they think about your product? These are important questions to ask yourself if you want to keep them happy and coming back for more. So, let's list something they care about. Go ahead and fill in the blank with what your audience truly care about.

_____

_____

_____

_____

Now, let's brainstorm a way we can change something about our work to satisfy their need. How can we satisfy them in this area?

_____

_____

_____

_____

Do this exercise multiple times, and watch the benefits roll in. But what if your creative problem solving task doesn't involve an audience? No worries, my friend. There's another way.

Get super focused on one single detail. Pick a tiny, seemingly insignificant detail and just let your mind run wild from there. Let's say you're designing a solar panel. Focus on one single feature of its construction, such as its frame. Consider it. Think about what you like about it and how it's different from other frames. Zero in on that aspect and ask yourself what could transform this feature so that it was perfectly suited for a highly specific use?

Remember to finish this particular approach off by asking, "what have I not yet considered?"

14 WHAT WOULD MY HERO DO?

"I don't want to get to the end of my life and find that I just lived the length of it. I want to live the width of it as well."

Diane Ackerman

Listen up, peeps! You know those people who just get it right? They're smashing it out there, and we're all like "Wow! Look at them go!" But how much do we really know about them? Like, what was really going on behind the scenes? How did they start out when they were just a hot mess express? And most importantly, what specific things did they learn along the way to get where they are now?

So, let's take a closer look at these heroes of ours. Imagine them doing their thing, crushing it like a boss. And then ask yourself, "If they were in my shoes, what would they do in this very situation? And why am I not doing that already?" Don't be afraid to get all up in their business, people!

Now, some of you may have heroes like Einstein. And sure, he was a genius, but he had methods, people! He would visualize problems using detailed, vivid mental images, and then explore hypothetical scenarios with his "Gedankenexperiment"—thought experiments, if you will. He would even spend a decent chunk of time on these activities! And the key was to make things simple. So, if Einstein were here today with all the fancy technology we have, he would probably use all the creative tools around him to visualize and explain problems. He's still Einstein, but he's modern-day Einstein!

But you don't have to have the biggest, baddest hero out there. It could be someone in your field that you admire, who's doing things right. And once you know them a bit, you can put them in your current situation and ask yourself, "What would they do?" It's like having a little imaginary friend that's super smart and helpful!

Let's try it out, shall we?

Who's your hero in this situation? Don't be shy, fill in the blank.

_____

_____

_____

_____

What methods did they use to get where they are now? Get specific, people!

_____

_____

_____

_____

And finally, in your current situation, what would they do? Think about it, people!

_____

_____

_____

_____

Now get out there and channel your hero like the boss you are! Boom!

CONGRATULATIONS

Wow.

Wow, look at you! You've taken fourteen steps and made a significant milestone. Impressive! Take a moment to celebrate yourself, pump your fists, and feel good. Don't forget to do this for every activity you complete because it's all about building momentum. You have to keep that positive energy going!

Now, let's get serious. We're about to dive into the hurdle week, the tough third quarter of this book. The first quarter is always easy and fun, and the last quarter has the countdown to the finish line pushing you forward. But that pesky third quarter? It's a doozy. Low energy, pain, and no end in sight. So, you have to channel your inner professional and show up for your craft every day. Turn up, get on with it, and treat it with the respect it deserves.

And let's not forget the idea of becoming a professional. Take your creative pursuits seriously, like it's your job. Because, guess what? It is your job! You must take it seriously if you want to succeed. So, let's do this! Get ready for the hurdle week, and remember to celebrate your progress along the way. You got this!

15 STOP BEING SUCH A HARSH CRITIC—PART 1

"I am my own experiment. I am my own work of art."

Madonna

Hey there! Are you ready to have more fun so you can enjoy not just the outcome but the process itself?

First things first: Let's talk about punishment. If you beat yourself up every time you sit down to be creative, do you think you're going to keep coming back? Nope, you're going to avoid it like the plague. So, be kind to yourself and enjoy the process.

Now, enjoying the process is much easier said than done. You can't enjoy something if you don't know how to do it, right? It's like playing tennis for the first time and not knowing how to hit the ball over the net. You're not going to have fun if you're just frustrated and clueless.

So, learn the damn process! Break it down into parts and label them in your head. From writing a paragraph to editing a chapter, each step is important and interesting in its own way. Don't just begrudgingly perform them, embrace them!

Let's do an exercise to help you get started. Separate your creative activity into three parts.

_____

_____

_____

_____

Got it? Good. Now, take one of those parts and break it down into three distinct parts that occur within it. For example, if you're researching, there's typing words into Google or a Chatbot, copying and pasting elements, and choosing what to include. See, it's not just one big mess!

_____

_____

_____

_____

Now, whenever you're doing these parts, be kind to yourself and observe what you're doing as an integral step to creative mastery. Even the smallest amount of progress is progress, so give yourself a pat on the back. And remember, each tiny part is a skill that you can get better at.

So, it's time to fall in love with the process! I'm not talking about falling in love with a hottie (although that's always a bonus), I'm talking about labeling every single step of the way as a skill you're improving. Every little thing counts, people! And when you see the progress you're making, it's like fireworks going off in your brain.

So, go ahead and start falling in love with each little part. It's like falling in love with a sport. You learn the moves, practice, and get better over time.

16 STOP BEING SUCH A HARSH CRITIC—PART 2

"Nothing is ugly as long as it is alive."

Coco Chanel

Ok, time to learn how to be nice to yourself!

But listen up, my dear harsh critics, it's time to give ourselves a break. We need to stop judging ourselves and our work as being terrible. That's just a stage in the process of becoming great. So let's stop putting ourselves down and holding ourselves to impossible standards. Don't be a jerk to yourself. Don't call yourself names or say mean things. You're not going to get anywhere by being a bully. Trust me, I tried it and it didn't work out so well.

And for the love of all that is good and holy, take a dang break once in a while! Rest is important, y'all.

Remember, everything starts off a bit rubbish until you put in some hard work and toil. Don't compare yourself to others who have been doing this for ages or who have natural strengths for some style that's not your forte. And don't stress yourself out about it either. That kind of worrying isn't going to help you get any better.

So let's focus on the good things, shall we? Think about something you've done that you love. Even if you see the imperfections (gasp!).

Write what that is here.

_____

_____

_____

_____

Pick out the thing you love about it. Write it down, folks!

_____

_____

_____

_____

And take a moment to appreciate how that instance above shows a development of your skills over time. Yes, even those rusty skills count.

Being a harsh critic often stops us from trying to improve, so let's ditch that mentality and find the good in our work. Embrace the struggle, my friends. That's what makes the process so darn exciting.

17 ARE YOU USING THESE THREE LOGICAL STEPS?

"You have brains in your head. You have feet in your shoes. You can steer yourself any direction you choose."

Dr. Seuss

Let's go through the most logical steps to a creative project.
Step 1: What is the Problem?
Alright, let's state the problem here.

_____

_____

_____

___

Now, give me more juice on that problem, get more specific here.

___
___
___
___

Excellent job, you are a star. Now, let's do it one more time. When it comes to writing a novel, for example, the problem could be stated as, "How do I write a romance novel that'll make teenage girls swoon? What would make them melt?" But let's spice it up even more with specificity, like "How do I learn to write a romance novel that will make girls go ga-ga in the next 12 months, and what's the quickest way to test if I'm doing it right?"

By adding in time constraints and quantitative requirements, you can set a more detailed and specific problem. That presents some answers, doesn't it? It might even present as a completely different question, which, in this case, is about learning the skill itself and the process of learning the skill.

If you did it once already, try it again now.

State your problem simply.

___

_____

_____

_____

State your problem more specifically.

_____

_____

_____

_____

Step 2: What's the Uncomfortable Thing You're Not Admitting?

Now, we need to come up with solutions by asking: "What's an uncomfortable thing I'm not admitting that I'll need to do in order to solve that challenge?" This helps you uncover the information that you know, but for some reason, is a bit uncomfortable to face. There's always some information hidden in there.

Write what the uncomfortable thing you're not admitting is that you'll need to do in order to solve your challenge.

_____

_____

_____

_____

So, take a moment to reflect on the changes that you'll have to make to your approach that you're putting off making, but will make a huge impact. With writing a romance novel, it might be incredibly hard to admit that you'd have to take a whole course on writing. But if you ask yourself, it might possibly be the fastest route to go from average to good. There might actually not be a faster way through, even if you wish there was. Especially in this case, if you asked, "where else are the lessons going to come from?"

To convince yourself to take the harder, slower path, you can ask the question, "realistically, how else am I going to achieve X or improve Y?"

18 WHAT LESSONS CAN YOU APPLY FROM YOUR PAST?

"Experience is not what happens to you; it's what you do with what happens to you."

Aldous Huxley

Now, I know what you're thinking, "I don't want to solve problems, I just want to eat cake and watch Netflix." But trust me, life is full of obstacles and we must tackle 'em head-on.

Think back, way back. Maybe you were a tiny tot or a moody teenager, or hey, maybe you're already a grown-ass adult. Either way, I know you've solved something in your life. It could be a relationship issue, a physical challenge, or a practical problem. The bigger the better, folks. Got the problem in mind? Write it here.

_____

_____

_____

_____

Now, think about how you tackled that problem. Did you need to channel your inner superhero? Did you call on the wisdom of Beyoncé? Whatever it was, I want you to get specific about what helped you overcome that obstacle. What lesson did you learn? Jot it down, my friends.

_____

_____

_____

_____

But here's the thing, we humans tend to make the same mistakes over and over. We forget the lessons we've learned and end up in the same pickle as before. That's why we're going to do a little 180 and think about a time when we failed. I know, I know, nobody likes to dwell on their failures. But let's be real, we learn a lot from our mistakes and missteps.

So think about a time when you tried something and it just didn't work out. Write it here.

_____

_____

_____

_____

What went wrong? What lesson did you learn from that experience?

Write the lesson you learned.

_____

_____

_____

_____

And most importantly, how can you apply that lesson to your current issue?

_____

_____

_____

You got this, guys. Remember, you're a problem-solving badass. Keep those lessons in your back pocket and tackle those obstacles like a boss.

19 WHAT IF YOU IMPOSED SEVERE CONSTRAINTS?

"Necessity is the mother of invention."

Plato

Let's talk about creativity and constraints. Weird combo, right? But trust me, it works.

Here's the deal, when we have too much freedom, our brains can get overwhelmed and we end up with subpar work. That's why imposing some strict constraints can actually help our creative juices flow.

Here are some key constraints you can consider imposing:

Let's start with time. You only have 30 minutes to come up with a finished product. That's it. No more time. So, what do you do? You get to work, baby! Use that 30 minutes wisely and see what you come up with. Then take the best from that and use it in your project. Boom! You just got more productive.

Now, let's narrow the focus. Don't try to solve the whole problem, just one small segment of it. What would need to be different and more specific about your creation in order to solve this narrower problem? Think about it, get creative.

Next, let's talk themes. What's a theme or concept that must be shown within your completed work? It absolutely must adhere to this new concept or theme, so that would change the nature of your work. How would that affect things? Get your thinking cap on and let your imagination run wild.

Collaboration can be key. If you're not working with someone yet, you have to. That's your constraint. How does that affect your work? Maybe you'll get new ideas, maybe you'll have to compromise, but either way, collaboration can be a great way to get those creative juices flowing.

There are tons of constraints. You can only use one color, only use five words, three materials, two locations, it could be anything. Write your constraints here.

_____

_____

_____

_____

Write how you're going to respond creatively to these new constraints.

_____

_____

_____

_____

Imposing constraints can set you free and help you create something amazing. Now, get to it!

20 PICTURE THE END GOAL BUT GET IT RIGHT

"A goal without a plan is just a wish."

Antoine de Saint-Exupéry

Hey there! Let's talk about success. You know, that thing we all want but can't quite put our finger on. Well, let's try to put our finger on it. Can you picture what success looks like? Can you see it in all its glory? Can you imagine the parts that make it up? Let's get specific here, people!

No matter what creative project you're working on, there are going to be a lot of elements that make it successful. So let's identify them now. Think about a successful song, for example. It might have a memorable chorus, a catchy lyric, a theme that resonates, a change in tempo, and a moment of exciting release.

Boom, five elements of success right there.

Now it's your turn. Think about your own creative work and come up with five elements of success.

Write them here.

_____

_____

_____

_____

_____

But wait, stop right there. Are you sure you're thinking about the right things? Are you focusing on what truly matters? Take a step back and revise your list. What are the five aspects of your work that truly matter?

_____

_____

_____

_____

_____

Got 'em? Good. Now pick one. Just one element that you think is crucial to your success. Project yourself into the future. What actions were necessary to produce that element? Did it happen smoothly and effortlessly? Come on, be honest, did it? Of course not! Nothing in art, science, or business is ever that easy. We all have this idea that creativity is like a bolt of lightning striking us, but the truth is, it's a lot of focused development work to get there one piece at a time.

Write what got that element right.

_____

_____

_____

_____

You can do this for all the important parts of your work.

So now you have a more accurate picture of what success looks like and the steps to get there. The only thing standing between you and that creation you seek is...what, exactly? Simply take the action that's required!

21 WHAT IF WE WROTE OUR OWN RULES?

"If you obey all the rules, you miss all the fun."

Katharine Hepburn

Who says we have to follow the same old boring rules that everyone else has been using? What if we threw caution to the wind and blazed our own trail?

Now, to do this, we can take rules from completely different domains and apply them to our own. It might sound crazy, but hear me out. Let's say we take the rules from a cooking competition and apply them to writing a novel. The rule for the cooking competition is to use a secret ingredient in each dish. So, for writing a novel, maybe we can have a secret plot twist that leaves the reader gasping for air?

But wait, hold on a sec! We can't just make up rules out of thin air. We need to find rules that are proven to work. So, let's analyze the rules from another domain in terms of what they're supposed to accomplish, or some other feature of the rules, and then apply that to our creative challenge.

So, what domain are you going to take the rules from? It could be anything, from the way a cat plays with a toy to the way your neighbor takes out the trash. Write it down here.

_____

_____

_____

_____

Now, let's figure out a way to express the rules. For example, if we're taking rules from the way a cat plays with a toy, the rule could be to always keep the toy moving and make sure it's never predictable. Express the rules.

_____

_____

_____

_____

Finally, how could these rules be applied to your creative challenge? For instance, if you're designing a website, you could use the cat's toy rule to make sure your website is interactive and engaging, with unexpected features that keep users on their toes. Write how the rules can be applied here.

_____

_____

_____

_____

Now, I know this might not be easy, but take the time to turn it over in your head until you come up with something interesting. Trust me, the results might surprise you!

3 WEEKS. INCREDIBLE.

All right, all right, all right! Can I just say, you are crushing it! Seriously, give yourself a round of applause. You deserve it! And let's be real, you're just getting started. There's a whole world of success waiting for you, my friend.

And as you keep building on your progress, you'll become a total creative powerhouse. People will be like, "Whoa, what happened to you? You're on fire!" And you'll just be like, "Yeah, I know. I did the work, baby."

But let's not forget, being creative isn't just about feeling good. It's about developing good habits and routines that help you consistently produce amazing work.

But if you've found even one activity that helps, make sure you share your new insights with those around you too. Creativity should not be a scarce resource—more is better. Help those around you also learn to think more creatively.

We're about to take things up a notch with some killer techniques that will elevate your creative game to a whole new level. Are you ready for this? Because I'm about to drop some serious knowledge on you. Let's do this!

22 IDENTIFY YOUR PROBLEM. MAKE IT AN OPPORTUNITY.

"Every problem is a gift. Without them, we wouldn't grow."

Tony Robbins

We've all got that one thing that's blocking our path, that thing we just can't seem to get past. Maybe it's a person, a situation, or just a nagging feeling in our heads. But guess what? We're about to flip the script and turn that obstacle into a secret weapon!

First things first, identify that pesky thing in your way. You know, the thing that makes you go "ugh, if only I could get rid of this, I could finally achieve my dreams!" Got it? Good. Write it here.

_____

_____

_____

Now, here's the fun part. We're going to change the way we look at it. Instead of seeing it as a blocker, we're going to see it as an opportunity to innovate and come up with a unique solution. That's right, we're going to take that negative energy and turn it into a jet pack boost to success!

Think about it, that thing that's blocking you is just a physical feature of the world. It's neither good nor bad objectively speaking. The judgment only exists in our brains. So let's reject that judgment and make it work for us instead.

Here's how to do it: ask yourself "What if...?" What if this obstacle actually forces me to adapt and change my approach? How can I use it to my advantage? Write down your answers and watch as that thing you thought was holding you back becomes your competitive advantage!

So, in what way might this obstacle force you to adapt to either use it, or fundamentally change how you do things?

_____

_____

_____

Once you've got this new way of operating, enforce it like it's nobody's business. Celebrate every little win and watch as your secret weapon becomes your go-to move for success.

So go ahead, embrace that obstacle and turn it into your biggest strength.

23 BE THE HARSHEST CRITIC YOU CAN IMAGINE

"Criticism, like rain, should be gentle enough to nourish a man's growth without destroying his roots."

Frank A. Clark

Alright, you aspiring critics, listen up! Today we're going to talk about how to become a dispassionate observer and a neutral detective of your own work. Yeah, I know, it sounds like something straight out of CSI, but trust me, it's the only way to make your work stand out from the crowd.

So, what does it mean to become a harsh critic? Well, it means you have to assess your work objectively, even if it hurts your precious ego. That's right, your feelings are not the point here, making your work good is. And to do that, you have to detach yourself from it, like it was someone else's work.

Now, I know it sounds good in theory, but can you actually do it? The answer is: probably not. You have to go through the painful process of getting feedback from others first. And trust me, they're not going to say your work is the greatest thing they've ever witnessed. That's just not how it works, people!

So, if you've never had feedback before, brace yourself, because it's going to be uncomfortable. But don't worry, you have to start somewhere, right? Get someone you trust to critique your work and be honest about it. Ask them what they like about it, and more importantly, what they don't like. Yeah, it's going to sting a bit, but it's worth it. Because every ounce of feedback you get makes you stronger and better.

So write who you're going to get to give you critical feedback.

_____

_____

_____

_____

And here's the thing, as you grow as an artist or professional, you'll get better at taking feedback. You'll learn to adapt and integrate it into your own knowledge and insights. But you'll always need external people to give you insights, because sometimes it's hard to see your work as other people will see it. So, keep asking for feedback, and keep learning from it.

Now something that might help here is to imagine what

feedback might they give? What might they critique?
Write your guess here.

_____

_____

_____

_____

Now, obviously do not bias them by telling them this ahead of time! Let them give you feedback and just see what they say.

And remember, your work is for other people, not for you. You're creating it so others can enjoy it, use it, or benefit from it. So, don't let your ego get in the way of making it the best it can be. Now, go forth and become the harshest critic of your own work!

24 WHAT COULD MAKE THIS SO GOOD, PEOPLE WILL WONDER HOW THEY LIVED WITHOUT IT?

"If you build it, they will come."

Kevin Costner, Field of Dreams

Alrighty then, folks! We've got ourselves one heck of a prompt here! It's like the holy grail of creativity. But, hold on to your pants, it might not work for everything, like designing a rocket engine component, unless you can reframe it as "What could make this so good, the engine will wonder how it lived without it?" Boom, problem solved!

However, for a whole lot of other creative projects, this prompt is absolutely golden. I'm talking about everything from songs to books, pictures to products, events, you name it! So, let's give it a go, shall we?

The prompt is: What could make this so good, people will wonder how they lived without it?

Now the key to this is to consider that this would mean your work is now so useful to them that they'll keep coming back to it, telling their friends about it, and spreading the word. It's so damn good that the old way of doing things is as outdated as a flip phone.

It replaces something in their life with something so much more useful for fulfilling a deep need that they'd never consider going back. It would be a great step backwards now.

Let's try it again. Imagine your creation has changed someone's life so much that they can't even believe it. It's like magic, it's like sorcery, it's like a unicorn that poops rainbows. And now, you have to figure out the exact mechanism behind it.

Ask yourself: How has it changed the way they look at the world? How has it transformed a specific part of their life? How has it made their day-to-day activities easier or helped them accomplish a specific goal? Write that.

_____

_____

_____

_____

Let's get specific. How exactly has your creation achieved all of this? Has it made something faster and easier in a way that's not currently available? And if so, how have you done it? Write how it did it.

_____

_____

_____

_____

Give it a shot and fill in the blanks.
It's changed the way I:

_____

_____

_____

_____

And I will never go back to:

_____

_____

_____

_____

Because this new way:

_____

_____

_____

_____

Now, let's talk practicality. We have to situate our thoughts in reality, folks. Your new creation isn't going to suddenly make everyone fall in love with it. I mean, sure, a few people might, but you have to picture the way people already exist and interact with their environment. You have to insert your creation into their world and see what the best outcome is realistically.

So, first things first, identify what people are already doing in your realm. How are they solving the problem that you're about to solve? Write that here.

_____

_____

_____

_____

Alright, got it? Now, how are you going to come in and solve their problem so good that they'll never go back to the old way? Give us the deets.

_____

_____

_____

_____

And finally, why will they never go back to the old way? Give it to us straight.

_____

_____

_____

_____

For example: They'll never go back to the old way because my new painting fits so well with their décor and is such a conversation piece that it really stands out in a positive way.

One thing to keep in mind, though, is that we can't project what we want to be true onto reality. We might be wishing for something that isn't realistic or likely. So, think about the realistic scenario.

Here's a useful trick: Think about it as if it wasn't actually your work. Someone else has handed you their creation, and you have to ask yourself, "Is this going to change the way people do things, or will they stick with what they've got?" This is a high bar to climb, but it's worth the attempt.

25 WHERE ARE YOU SITUATED IN LIFE, CULTURE AND SOCIETY?

"Culture makes people understand each other better. And if they understand each other better in their soul, it is easier to overcome the economic and political barriers. But first, they have to understand that their neighbor is, in the end, just like them, with the same problems, the same questions."

Paulo Coelho

Alright folks, listen up because we're about to get real deep. Your work, your baby, your precious project, it's not just floating in a vacuum. No, it's part of a bigger picture, a social and cultural context, and it's time to reflect on how it fits in.

So, let's ask the tough questions, like are you making a real impact here? Or are you just another knock-off trying to be cool?

Don't be a wannabe, people, be a real change-maker.

But how do you do that? Well, let's start by looking at what's going on in the world around you. What issues are people facing? Who's getting left behind? What's the current political climate like? We're talking history, art, science, technology, you name it.

Once you've got a good grasp on the context, you can start to see where your work fits in. How is it contributing to the greater good? How is it making a difference in the areas that matter most? And here's the kicker, how is it doing this in a way that's so kick-ass, other people are going to want to write about it?

Now, I'm not just talking about some vague, abstract contribution here. We need to get specific. How is your work making a real impact in the current social-cultural context, and through what exact mechanism is it doing so? Write that here.

_____

_____

_____

_____

So, there you have it, folks. Take a good, hard look at the context around you, and then figure out how you can make a difference. Don't settle for mediocrity, be a force for change.

26 ARE YOU EXPERIENCING LIFE ENOUGH?

"The more that you read, the more things you will know. The more that you learn, the more places you'll go."

Dr. Seuss

Hey, you've made it this far, congrats! You must have something cooking up in that noggin of yours that's worth exploring. But hold up, before we get ahead of ourselves, let's take a moment to appreciate the beauty of the world around us. Look up at that big, blue sky, or take a gander at the horizon. And hey, if you're feeling adventurous, why not venture outside of your workspace and explore new places, new people, and new experiences?

Because let's face it, if you're just sitting around in your cubicle all day, your creative juices are going to be pretty stagnant. Your life experiences are the fuel that powers your ideas, and if you haven't had many, or if they've all been the same old boring routine, then you're going to struggle to come up with fresh ideas.

So ask yourself, are you experiencing enough different things? And if not, it's time to hit the road and explore! But don't worry, you don't have to have a specific plan. Sometimes the best adventures are the ones that are completely random and aimless. Just pick a direction and go.

27 IN THE UPCOMING JOURNEY, WHAT IS THE PINNACLE MOMENT?

"People will forget what you said, people will forget what you did, but people will never forget how you made them feel."

Maya Angelou

Alright, listen up, buttercups. We're talking about the big O here, and I don't mean Oprah. We're talking about the pinnacle moment, the climax, the grand finale. It doesn't matter if you're designing a new app or a fancy t-shirt, every great work builds up to that one moment that makes it all worth it.

So, what's your moment? What's the pièce de résistance that makes your project stand out? It's time to figure it out and own it. Put it here.

_____

_____

_____

_____

Let's break it down. In a book or movie, it's usually the epic battle or jaw-dropping revelation. Think "Avengers: Endgame"—the whole movie leads up to the final showdown with Thanos. In game design, there's always a final boss battle that's supported by smaller battles leading up to it. Even in music, there's a clear peak emotional moment, like a killer guitar solo or an epic chorus.

So, what's your moment? Identify it and then ask yourself: how does the rest of the project support it? You need to make sure that everything else in your work is leading up to that one grand moment, whether it's removing unnecessary product details to support the important component, or having a solid frame to support your magnificent rooftop.

So write how the rest of your work supports your pinnacle moment.

_____

_____

_____

_____

And get to work on supporting the pinnacle. Let's make it the grandest, most satisfying climax of your life.

28 AM I CONNECTING TO OTHERS ON AN EMOTIONAL LEVEL?

"I think I have learned that the best way to lift one's self up is to help someone else."

Booker T. Washington

Maybe this is less good for building, say, part of a new oven, if it's just one component. But if you're talking about the whole oven, then hell yes you can be talking about connecting to people on an emotional level. The whole oven experience will appeal to them.

If you're talking about a piece of code for a B2B financial payments software, then you still have an audience of customers, and users, and the experience should talk to them on an emotional level. It should, in this case, be so functionally easy, and so without errors, ever, that it makes them happy to use it.

Now, with a lot of other work it is far easier to see the importance of having some emotional connection, of some description, with your audience.

To do this, you need to know something about your audience. Not just something. But everything.

You need to know what makes them tick and what gives them, and not some other subsection of the population, an emotional rush, unique to what they care about.

What triggers already lie in their head, trigger words or memories or ideas or themes, that will perk their attention up. And what story can you tell or communicate that will tug at their hearts and minds?

What experience can you give them, that only comes from you, is noticeably linked to what you're providing and nowhere else, and that they want again and again?

Let's go through these steps now

Who is my audience

_____

_____

_____

_____

And who is an example of who my audience is not, and who I might actually want to repel—if you're attracting everyone, you're attracting no one specifically enough.

_____

_____

_____

_____

Now what gets them out of bed in the morning, where this item is concerned. What floats their boat where this category or thing is concerned.

_____

_____

_____

_____

Now, how do I float their boat, in a way that is noticeably different from everyone else.

_____

_____

_____

_____

What makes it completely impossible for them to forget this experience?

_____

_____

_____

_____

AWESOME

Twenty-eight giant creative leaps behind you and well done. Two more to go, till you hit the thirty. The emotional end is in sight.

Have you spread your newfound creativity around yet? Have you taken others through these exercises and let them try out new creative ways to think?

29 HAVE YOU OVERCOME YOUR SELF-DOUBT?

"If you hear a voice within you say 'you cannot paint,' then by all means paint and that voice will be silenced."

Vincent Van Gogh

Maybe you feel like you have no self doubt at all. Or maybe you are crippled by it. Hopefully you have used, by this point, the small simple steps to produce new ways of looking at the world. But not just new ways of looking at the world, specifically, and this is highly important, new ways of looking at your craft.

Because that is what you should be looking at, all throughout this, your craft.

Because it is yours.

It is your one.

One that you have.

It is attached to you.

And you are attached to the pursuit of it.

By breaking it down into smaller components you can see the elements that make up your craft.

By labelling them you can see the parts that are enjoyable, the tiny individual moves, that are enjoyable to get better at time by time.

And the room for self doubt, well, that shouldn't come up.

It's not about thinking about yourself or whether you're worth it or not (of course you are).

It's about finding the love of the very simple everyday parts of your task.

And that is what it is about.

It's such a subtle shift.

But it is also earth-shatteringly huge.

I guess it can be the sort of thing you don't believe exists until you are well and truly on the other side of it. And the doubt has gone. And all that is left is shining belief.

Maybe, for a lot of people, you need to start by boosting your self-belief.

In case you need to, let's do it quickly.

I believe that I am fully capable of:

_____

_____

_____

_____

I have already shown the progress towards this by:

_____

_____

_____

_____

This proves that my progress is heading in the direction, whereby, I will be fully capable of:

_____

_____

_____

_____

within a matter of weeks, months or years.

Any way I look at it, I am headed that way. I might already be further than I think.

The next steps I'm going to take on this journey, to indicate that I am heading in the right direction is to:

_____

_____

_____

_____

And when it gets hard, I know to do the smallest possible positive action that can help towards my goals, and so when it gets tough I will:

_____

_____

_____

_____

And when I complete each of the tiny steps, whether they have taken me ten seconds or two weeks, I will celebrate each time each step is made. This celebration will largely be internal, but I will feel the celebration and the joy from each positive step I make.

This will now be the contract that I make with myself.

My signature:

_____

30 JOYFUL DAYS OF CREATIVITY

_____

_____

_____

30 ARE YOU BEING KIND TO OTHERS?

"You can never do a kindness too soon, for you never know how soon it will be too late."

Ralph Waldo Emerson

Well, well, well, look who's here! It's you, you beautiful creative soul, you! And let me tell you, there's nothing more strange than finding a chapter about being kind to others in a book about creativity. But hey, we'll take it, won't we?

Now, let's get real, no one can make it to the top all by themselves, especially us creative folks who need others to help us navigate through our journeys. So, if you want to sail towards creative success, you have to show some love and energy towards building positive relationships in your life that will support your creativity. Who's got your back right now? Think about it. And don't forget, the stronger and larger your network is, the more your creativity will thrive.

Let's get personal, baby. Let's name some important people in your life who you would like to show more kindness towards.

_____

_____

_____

_____

Alright, now that you've got your crew, it's time to give back! Show some love, do something nice for them, no matter how small. Even if it's just replying to a message, because every little bit counts. Write here what you might do to be kind to them.

_____

_____

_____

_____

CONGRATULATIONS

Boom! Look at you, crushed it! But remember, creativity is a long game, baby. It's not just about one day, it's about making creativity a part of your everyday routine. Yeah, I know, routine sounds boring, but hear me out. Your life is a series of days, and how you live them is what matters. So, you want to be that creative badass who has the best daily routines and sticks with it, day in and day out.

Don't worry if you're not there yet, it takes time. 30 days might be enough, or maybe it'll take more. But hey, if you've made it this far, your leaps and bounds ahead.

Now take this first step, this first leap of progress, and build.

BONUS SECTION

So, you want some extra credit? Well, aren't you an overachiever! Here are a few more creativity boosters to try.

31 MAKING IT FOR THE KIDS

Imagine you're making your creation for kids. And not just any kids, but tiny little baby monkeys. How would you simplify your ideas? How would you make it easy for them to understand? This exercise will help you strip away all the unnecessary fluff and get to the core of what you're trying to create. Plus, who doesn't love imagining cute little baby monkeys enjoying their creations?

What would I do to make it so simple and fun a child would love it?

_____

_____

_____

_____

32 WHAT ARE THE KEY INGREDIENTS?

You know that recipe you've been working on perfecting? What's missing? Maybe it's a pinch of sass, or a dash of whimsy. Or perhaps you need to add some Beyoncé-level confidence. Whatever it is, figure it out and give it a try.

Write what ingredients will make your work absolutely stand-out excellent.

_____

_____

_____

_____

33 THE MOST AMAZING THING

Imagine the most amazing thing that's yet to happen in your creative journey. Maybe it's winning an award or getting a standing ovation. Maybe it's having your creation go viral and being shared all over social media. Whatever it is, close your eyes and picture it. And then, go out and make it happen!

The most amazing thing to come is:

_____

_____

_____

_____

www.ingramcontent.com/pod-product-compliance
Lightning Source LLC
Chambersburg PA
CBHW031430210526
45464CB00005B/2141